Microsoft Windows Repair Book

Remove Viruses & Passwords in Minutes!!

Plus: How to Reset Any Computer to Factory Default Condition by Manufacturer!

BEANIE L. YVONNE

ISBN-13:
978-1500227371

ISBN-10:
1500227374

To the loving memory of

Betty Allen, my friend and my companion...........

Table of Content

Introduction

This book contains the *essential* knowledge for repairing your computer like the Pros - from virus removal to optimizing (tweaking) your Windows computer's performance. You will also learn what the Pros know and what they don't want you to know. I will take you step by step through the process of removing login passwords to resetting your Window computer back to new out of box condition. The best part of choosing to buy this book is that all of the information I am going to share with you will cost you $0! That's correct, once you know how simple it is to repair your own computer, you will never pay someone else to do it for you again. In fact, once you're done reading this book I promise you'll start working on every computer that you've ever shoved into the closet. I wrote this book to spread the knowledge of computer repair and to debunk the myth that it costs hundreds of dollars to repair a computer. The vast majority of businesses are in business in the first place to make money…let's face it!

Case in point, I work alongside others that repair cell phones and televisions where I'm known as "The Computer Person." Ok, so anyway, you may or may not be familiar with those computer repair facilities that like to charge an arm and a leg for simple virus removal. Well, I have personally received hundreds of computers for repair from customers that have gone to places like "The Geek Squad." I have reason to believe some customers have been there and have run away because I can see those red stickers on the bottom and sides of their computer saying so. Anyway, I know you've seen those commercials where they dress up like the Nerds or Geeks and come out to your house and business to fix your computers. Yeah well, that's all good, fine and dandy, but what they don't tell you is that you're going to have to give them a kidney or lung in the process. If you don't believe me then check it out for yourself, go to the Geek Squad's website (Geeksquad.com) to view the costs involved for something as simple as what I'm going to show you how to do, *b*ut it's all free! You won't need to purchase anything-*ever*.

In today's economy, the average person must watch how and where they spend money; it's here today and gone tomorrow. This is especially true for the working class person that literally lives paycheck to paycheck, where a relatively minor occurrence could mean whether or not the light bill gets paid. The majority of people struggling today don't just have money laying around waiting to be handed over to someone or some company for something we can do for ourselves. Having said that, and without further ado, I would like to welcome you to the beginning of what should be a new perspective about computer repair.

Chapter 1:

Understanding Computer Viruses

Every since the beginning of the computer era, for both home and office, there has been a never-ending battle between sophisticated hackers and the PC (personal computer) end user. A computer virus or simply "virus" begins with a program code made to complete many simple yet damaging tasks. The code written is a type of Malware that, when executed, replicates by inserting copies of its program (like a human virus) into all existing programs, files, and even the boot section of the hard drive. One of primary goals of a computer hacker is to gain access to important information, whether stored or typed, about the end user's financial records and/or passwords. Other purposes for which viruses are spread into unsuspecting computer system could also be for political reasons or just simply to create havoc within a database; the reasons are limitless.

Computer hackers or "hackers" often look for vulnerabilities which may exist within an operating system to exploit and gain access to confidential information. As a matter of fact, commercial networking computer systems make up the large majority of attacks. As recently as the last quarter of 2013, Target Corporation, which is a clothing store chain, was hacked and over 110 million customer's had their names, home addresses, email addresses, and passwords stolen right from the corporate database. As you can see, even the largest of corporations are not exempt from virus attacks that often cripple entire networks.

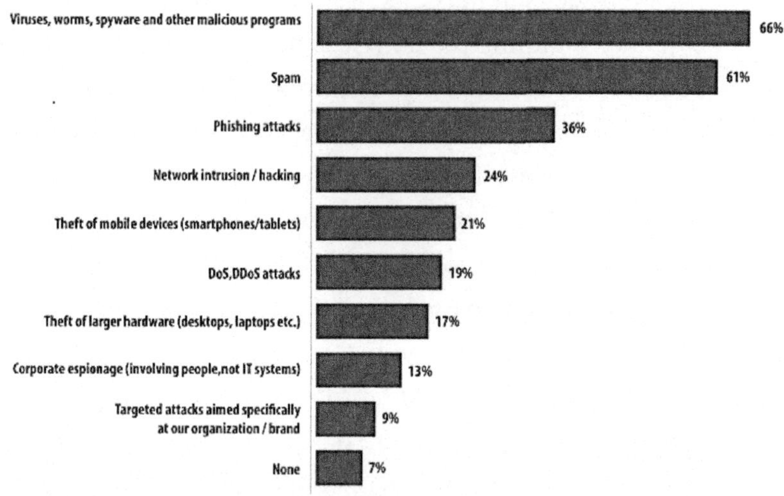

Figure: 1-1 A survey by Kaspersky Lab and B2B International found that 91% of organizations had a significant cyber-attack within a 12 month period, and 9% were victims of targeted attacks.

There are no such things as fully protected computer networks that are hacker-proof, no matter how hard we try, there are always exploitable loopholes. Microsoft realizes this very real threat, which is why so many different vulnerability patches are sent to its end user by way of security updates. **Windows updates** are designed to fix security flaws that hackers could utilize to gain access through a backdoor, so to speak, into your computer system. Updates alone can't protect your operating system from cyber-attacks, there should always be multiple layers of protection in place to minimize risks. An antivirus programs provides such a barrier and a secondary line of defense. A virus program seeks to mask its presence upon gaining entry by essentially fooling the antivirus program and terminating the ability to update its virus definition database. Computer viruses cause billions of dollars in damage yearly by corrupting operating systems and causing complete system failures.

Computer viruses can hide in many places within any operating system such as links, boot sectors, any file folder, email attachments, and even memory modules. Chances are if you have a suspicion that your computer is running slow or you are having pop-ups with ads then you probably do have a virus. A usual side effect of an infection is that programs tend to open much slower than usual, even failing to open all together. Then again, there might be different explanations behind a delayed response, including a hard drive that needs defragmentation, a computer that needs more memory (RAM), or the presence of more than one antivirus program conflicting.

Having said that, no existing antivirus program will make your computer 100% secure; IT security specialists are always looking for better approaches to tackle the current and emerging threats that exist today. One method of hunting for current virus programs within a computer network is by compiling a database of all known virus names and attributes. The virus definition updates are performed automatically when you have a good antivirus program like AVAST! (Free edition).

There are other antivirus programs out there that work just as good, but all programs aren't the same. Just be sure that whatever antivirus software you choose, offers a real-time protection shield. A good rule of thumb is that there should only be one antivirus program running at a time that provides real-time protection. The logic behind this principle is that having two or more antivirus protection programs running at the same time will only slow your overall computer's performance by scanning and then rescanning the same files, thus hindering its ability to efficiently protect itself.

Antivirus programs have the simple task of scanning documents and monitoring for suspicious activities that may be running in the background or behind the scenes. If one antivirus program scans a file and then releases it, then the next antivirus program will scan that same file again – and so on and so on. Scanning a document multiple times may effectively cause your computer to use too much of its allocated CPU (Central Processing Unit) processing power, while creating all sorts of unnecessary program hang-ups. The worst case scenario arising from a CPU running at full speed constantly is that the computer will run hot and begin to overheat the tiny chips contained within the motherboard. The computer's fan is meant to aid in keeping vital components from reaching critical temperatures, but these miniature cooling fans have their limitations. A computer infected with a virus will almost always raise the CPU usage to critical levels, sometimes even causing the infamous "blue screen of death." (Illustration 1-2)

Figure 1-2: Computer crash illustration

Common Types of Computer Infections

A virus will most certainly thrive in a computer host that doesn't have a strong defense to protect against it. The most common types of computer infections are: Trojans, Botnets, Web Browser, and Scareware. All of which only represent the smallest fraction of computer viruses circulating around the internet today. All viruses are considered bad and they are made with a specific function and task to accomplish. There are, however, some computer viruses that are much worse than others.

Trojans are designed to run on your system with the least amount of obstruction to your day to day activities, making this particular virus harder to detect. The basic nature of a Trojan is that it gives the appearance of a humble program that means you no harm. However, it's *au contraire Mon Cheri*.....quite the opposite! Once this nasty bugger gets into your computer and dug in, it can cause all sorts of irreparable damage before you could even blink. A Trojan is basically a backdoor, establishing links between hacker and your computer from a remote location. Trojans by nature do not replicate themselves, but when active they implement malicious code that can cause the computer to run slower. Computer end users are often tricked into opening email attachments and by clicking on links within websites that contain the virus code. The main purpose of the Trojan is data theft or data corruption. There are other signs and symptoms of a Trojan such as: blue screen crashing (a.k.a blue screen of death), destroying and corrupting data, keystroke capturing (Keyboard seems unresponsive), webcam viewing, and denial of service to websites.

Botnets (a.k.a zombie computers) are computers that have been taken over to do the bidding of the remote hacker without you even suspecting it. Once your computer is compromised, it is then added to the collective of other computers that have also been infected to act as one large network. This zombie controlled network of computers can now reach out to other non-infected computers and servers by way of email, invites, or just by being connected to an unsecured networking system. The best defense if a good offense in where you never open email attachments from unknown sources and you scan email attachments with good antivirus software from sources you do know.

Scareware is another form of computer virus whereby the unsuspecting user is infected with a fake antivirus program that offers protection. Now this is where it becomes interesting because if you click to close out the fake antivirus message, that will actually initiate or start the programs launch. Many people have been duped into actually purchasing these fake antivirus programs and have literally handed over their credit card information for the hacker to steal. Scareware has become quite good these days at looking very official, just like the real thing.

However, you should never buy antivirus programs without knowing the source, which is can be easily verified by customer's reviews on the internet. There are many different types of computer viruses in this ever-changing world we live in today as, well as many different antivirus programs. There are certain things that you can do as an end user to ensure that you are protected, such as having an active firewall in place, ensuring Windows updates are current, having a good real-time antivirus program, and perform frequent personal password changes.

Web Browser Virus a.k.a Browser Hijacking Virus attacks web browsers such as Internet Explorer, Firefox, Mozilla, and Google Chrome. This purpose of this virus is to redirect the computer user from the original requested website to an advertised website which generates revenues by redirecting internet traffic forcefully. Oftentimes the unsuspecting person downloads the virus with is contained in a software package that the user wishes to install. When the user downloads the file and begins to install the program, the user often chooses to add various toolbars that actually house the virus. There are some pretty good antivirus programs out there that have named many of the hijacking search toolbars used in the internet redirecting scheme. A few toolbars that have been flagged as being potentially malicious are: **Cool Web Search, Conduit Search, and Babylon Search**. The best remedy for unintentional installations of unnecessary programs is to thoroughly read the options being presented. You should never just click, click, and click to advance the installation process nor should you always choose express installation. It is advisable to take your time when installing a program and choose custom installation so that you can uncheck any box authorizing unwanted programs.

How to Best Protect Your Computer

With the advent of Digital Subscriber Line (DSL), risk of cyber-attacks have risen dramatically. DSL allows a computer to remain connected to the internet 24hrs a day, 7 days a week, and 365 days per year. This, of course, allows the hacker plenty of time to work on getting into your computer's files while you sleep. That being said, you should begin to develop safe habits that will minimize the risks of having data stolen and files corrupted. Here are a few suggestions:

•Turning off your computer while not in use will leave a smaller window of opportunity for a hacker to gain access
•Perform regular windows updates
•Perform regular antivirus scans
•Ensure Windows Firewall is up and running
•Change your passwords monthly with combination of numbers, letters, and symbols
•Never open email attachments from anyone that you don't know
•Scan attachments before opening email from those you do know

You should take precaution by making sure to enable the pop-up blocker in all web browsers. Also, by optimizing your browser's security setting you can change how internet sites collect information about you and your browsing history. Most websites drop cookies, or tiny bits of encrypted data, into your computer's web browser to learn about your browsing behavior. Cookies record such thing as what images or text you click on or how long you stay on a particular web page. Cookies also collect and store credit card information, addresses, and even passwords. When the user returns to that same website, the cookie information is transmitted back to the website host's server informing it that you have returned.

The use of cookies for tracking has raised security and privacy concerns prompting The United States legislation to make laws governing the methodology by which website owners collect and store data of consumers. Another way of taking precautions is by ensuring that the User Account Control (UAC) is enabled, thus better protecting your computer from programs attempting to run without administrative privileges.

If the UAC feature is activated, the user will be prompted to either allow or terminate an application's request to execute, thereby potentially preventing unwanted programs from making changes to your settings. Beginning in Windows 7, users can change how often they are alerted to when a change is being made to the computer; you can control these setting in the UAC panel. It is often a good practice to sign in with a standard user account that has limited permissions to surf the web or access programs. The reasoning behind this practice is that a virus would need to infect an administrator account in order to gain access to the areas of a computer that could actually cause any real harm. The important thing to remember is that as an administrator, you will have control of whether you want to allow a program to install or not, which is an important step in stopping a potential virus attack in its tracks.

Chapter Summary

There are several tasks that you can accomplish to safeguard your computer network from the threat of cyber attacks, updating your security settings and frequently changing your passwords are a good start. Surfing the internet without proper antivirus protection will dramatically increase the risk of your computer becoming infected with malicious code. You should install a good antivirus program and always make sure that your operating system is current with all its security updates. Windows Updates are used to seal security breaches that hackers may attempt to exploit to gain access to computer databases; hackers are becoming more and more resourceful. Routine security scans should also be performed with your trusted antivirus program, both boot scan and full system scans should be scheduled regularly.

Emails are risky, never open email from anyone that you don't know and always scan email attachments from those you do know. Developing and practicing good preventative methods like completely turning off your computers while not in use, as well as using a Standard account instead of an Administrative account also helps to minimize risks. If you choose to install a program, don't just click, click, and click all the way through. Be sure read all fine print in the details because more times than not, you will probably be installing extra programs or bloatware without even knowing it. A good tip is to use the customized installation choice, allowing you to see exactly what's being installed or whether or not you want or even need those optional third party programs contained within. Enable all popup blockers in your web browsers and make sure that your User Account Control (UAC) is active; these are just a few of the things you can do to best protect your computer network. Always remember that the best defense against cyber attack is having a good offensive protocol.

Chapter 2:

Network Security

Most networks, home or office, are comprised of several integral components that have the tasks of sending and receiving internet signals. The first component, being the actual internet signal, is sent via cable from your Internet Service Provider (ISP) to the Cable Modem. Once the signals come in via modem, it is then routed through the modem into the wireless network router (optional). The wireless router then broadcasts the signal throughout the home or office, allowing anyone inside of your network with a password to connect to the internet. A secure network is only as strong as the weakest access point connected to that network. In other words, if you have several computers simultaneously running inside of your home or office network and one computer gets infected, then all computers could become infected. A method of infecting multiple computers within a network is by turning one of the computers into a botnet (computer zombie) where the infected computer acts as a host to the virus that can infect all other computers via file transfer.

Many computers today use Wi-Fi Protected Access (WPA or WPA2) instead of the older Wired Equivalent Privacy (WEP). **WEP** is a standard that came from the older 802.11 wireless networking protocol which was designed to provide the same type of internet security as the Local Area Network (LAN) which uses DSL line.WEP generates encrypted packets of data that transmit information from origin to destination, but with the technology of today WEP security has become outdated and could be easily compromised.

The most preferred security standard recommended is **WPA**, or **WPA2** which is stronger of the two. WPA and WPA2 authentication will work with all current wireless networks with a shared key that is created by the home or office network administrator. Aside from securing your networking system, passwords should be changed often as well as signing into your user account with a more restrictive account such as guest or standard user.

Changing Windows Passwords (Logged In)

Setting your password for all versions of windows is a relatively simple task. Beginning with earlier versions of Windows all the way through Windows 7, the Control Panel is the central hub for making changes to you user accounts. In later versions of Windows (8 and 8.1) we will be using the PC Settings folder to make changes to the user accounts.

Windows XP (*Same for earlier versions*)

•Navigate to **Control Panel** by clicking Start, then Control Panel, and finally User Accounts

•Open User Accounts menu

•Choose "Change my password" or "Create a password"

•Enter your current password if changing or enter a new password if none existing

•Enter new password in again (optionally you may choose to enter a password hint)

•Click "Change Password" if changing or "Create Password" if doing this for first time

Windows Vista and Windows 7

•Navigate to **Control Panel** by clicking Start, then Control Panel, and User Accounts and Family Safety

•Open User Accounts menu

•Choose "Change your password" or "Create a password"

•Enter your current password if changing or enter a new password if none existing

•Enter new password in again (optionally you may choose to enter a password hint)

•Click "Change Password" if changing or "Create Password" if doing this for first time

•Shortcut: Hold down Ctrl + Alt + Delete to enter Task Manager and choose "change a password"

Windows 8 and Windows 8.1

•Move the mouse or cursor to the right edge of your screen for "Charms Menu (Shortcut by choosing Windows + F key)

•Scroll down and choose "Settings" (Shortcut by choosing the Windows + I key)

•Navigate over to "Change PC Settings" and open it

•Navigate to "Users" and choose user

•Underneath "Sign in options" choose "Change your password"

•Once open, enter old password

•Now enter new password

•Finally re-enter new password.

The final screen should read "You've changed your password"

Note: Alternatively you may open the Search box and type "change password" for quicker access.

Remove Windows Passwords (Can't Login)

In this section I will show you how to remove login passwords from Windows in minutes. Follow these steps if you have ever been in a situation where you have forgotten your password or if you have purchased a computer from someone that has forgotten the password. I will show you a couple of different ways to go about getting into a password protected computer and deleting the old password.

Windows XP

•Start your computer normally and immediately hold down “F8” for 5 seconds and then release. *Note*: The F8 key is on the top row of your keyboard.

•The next screen you see will give you options of how to start Windows. Choose “Safe Mode.”

•Once Safe Mode screen appears proceed into it

•Click on Administrator account

•Once the account is logged into go to “Control Panel”

•Next go to “User Accounts”

•Choose the user account with the password

•Next choose “Delete Password”

•Save everything and exit the control panel

•Lastly, restart your computer and log into your original account

Windows Vista/Windows7/Windows8/Windows 8.1

If you are handy with a keyboard and are not afraid of making a mistake, then I have a shortcut to unlocking the hidden administrator account. Only an administrator has the authority to make changes to an existing Windows account or delete an account or password of any user. What happens if the administrator gets locked out? Well here's a simple backdoor that may work:

•Reboot the computer and as soon as it turns back on, press and hold the "**F8**" key (5 seconds).

•The next screen will appear and choose "**safe mode with command prompt**"

•When the command prompt appears, type: **net user administrator /active: yes**

•The command completed successfully message should now be visible

•Restart the computer and now the new "Administrator" account will be next to the original at the Windows sign in screen

Lastly, enter the Administrator account and proceed to control panel to delete password, which is located in User Accounts and Family Safety. Choose user account to delete the password. In the event that the above didn't work then the Administrator account may already be activated and was renamed to the currently named account. At any rate if you weren't successful then go to the next step of downloading the needed program

For users that are running Windows Vista, 7, 8, and 8.1, all you will have to do is download the following free Windows password reset program to a computer that you can log into. If you don't have a computer that you can log into there is always the option of your local library. Once you have downloaded the program to your computer, you will next have to copy the files to a blank CDR or USB drive. Follow these steps: Navigate to your web browser and download the Free Windows Password Reset Tool at http://www.chntpw.com/download/

•Choose to download file cd140201.zip (for CD drive) If you have CD drive

•Choose to download file usb140201.zip (for USB drive) if you have no CD drive (Illustration 2-1)

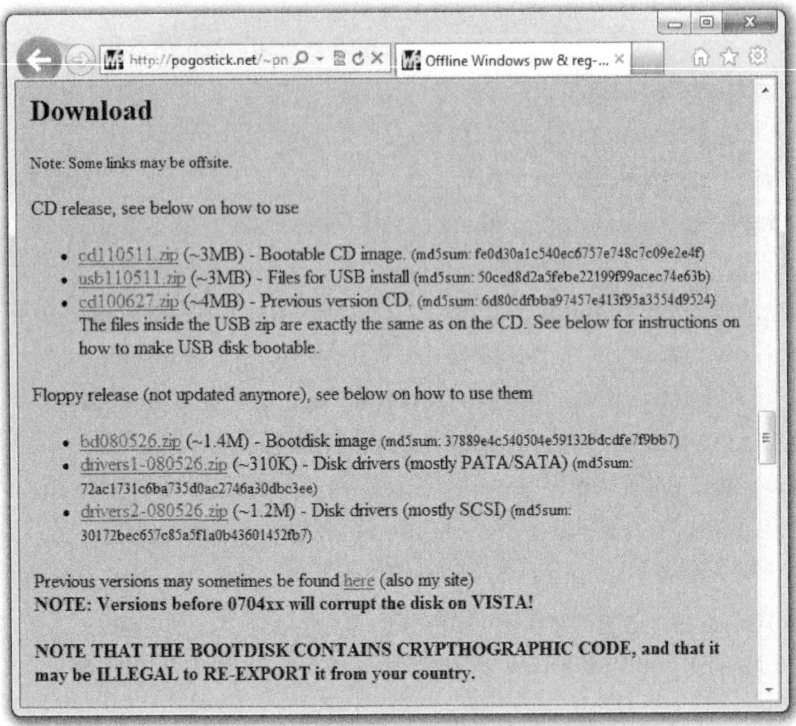

Illustration 2-1

•Navigate to the destination that you have downloaded the file to
•Right click on the file (which is in the form of a .zip) and choose "extract files"
•When the next box opens it will show a default location to where the files will be extracted to
•Click OK
•Navigate to the extracted file folder which will contain an ISO image (see Glossary of Terms) of the program

If you don't have a CDR burning program download and install Imgburn for free. If you are using a USB, you will need to make it bootable by downloading the free Microsoft tool and running the program. Point the installer to where the ISO file is located and then proceed down to "changing boot order" for your computer. Make sure the USB drive contains no files during this process. If your USB does contain files and you want to keep them, you must copy the files to another folder or onto your computer's desktop. To do this, just insert your USB flash drive into any computer and this should prompt Windows to give you a list of all files contained within. Now highlight all your files and drag them to whatever folder or location that you choose for safe keeping until you're done. Once you've completed the copying of documents or programs on the flash drive, go to http://www.microsoftstore.com/store/msusa/html/pbPage.Help_Win7_usbdvd_dwnTool to begin format and install the bootable USB program that will allow you to copy the password reset program tool.

Once on the website (for CD users) choose "Download Latest Version" on top right of screen and install. Run Imgburn (for CD users) to burn the ISO file image that you've downloaded and extracted before. The program will ask you for location of the ISO file and select that location. Insert the CD back into your computer once Imgburn has completed.

If you are unfamiliar with this process of changing your boot order, then you can just follow these simple instructions. For Asus, Acer, Gateway, Dell, HP, Compaq, and Toshiba press "F2" to change the boot order in bios. If your manufacture is not listed here then you will have to proceed to that manufacturer's website to find which key is used to change the boot order. Alternatively you can try "F10", "F9", or "F12"

•Once your computer is booted using your Disk or USB pen drive your screen should be in a generic black and white screen (Illustration 2-2)

```
***************************************************************************
*                                                                         *
*       Windows Reset Password / Registry Editor / Boot CD                *
*                                                                         *
*  (c) 1998-2011 Petter Nordahl-Hagen. Distributed under GNU GPL v2       *
*                                                                         *
* DISCLAIMER: THIS SOFTWARE COMES WITH ABSOLUTELY NO WARRANTIES!          *
*             THE AUTHOR CAN NOT BE HELD RESPONSIBLE FOR ANY DAMAGE       *
*             CAUSED BY THE (MIS)USE OF THIS SOFTWARE                     *
*                                                                         *
* More info at: http://pogostick.net/~pnh/ntpasswd/                       *
* Email       : pnh@pogostick.net                                         *
*                                                                         *
* CD build date: Wed May 11 20:16:09 CEST 2011                            *
***************************************************************************

Press enter to boot, or give linux kernel boot options first if needed.
Some that I have to use once in a while:
boot nousb         - to turn off USB if not used and it causes problems
boot irqpoll       - if some drivers hang with irq problem messages
boot vga=ask       - if you have problems with the videomode
boot nodrivers     - skip automatic disk driver loading

boot: _
```

Illustration 2-2

•Next you will choose to boot by pressing your enter key to initiate the automatic process

•Choose operating system partition (usually the one with the largest partition size) by pressing the corresponding number and then hitting the enter key (Illustration 2-3)

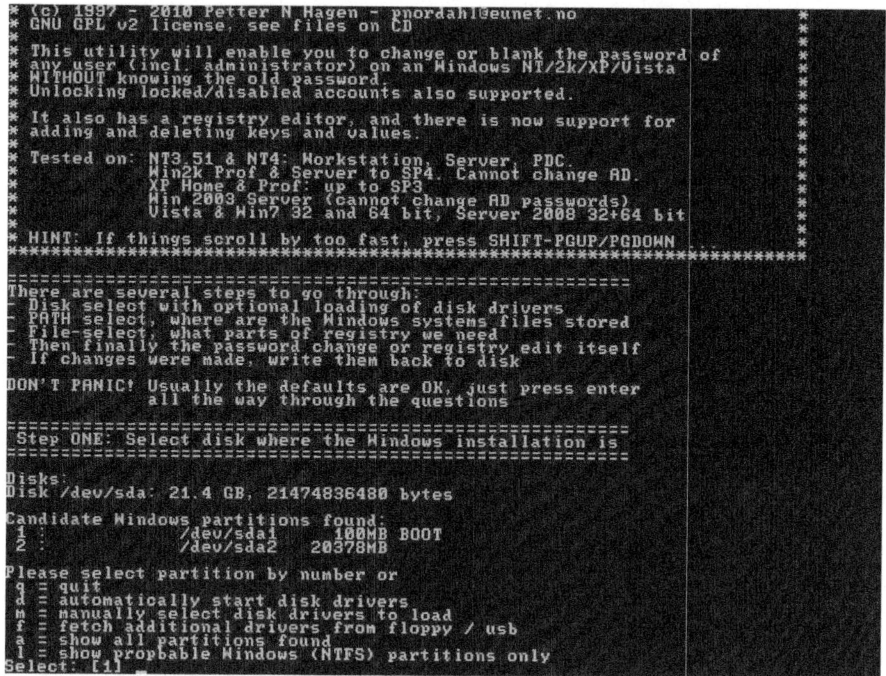

Illustration 2-3

•When the programs loads the chosen partition, you will next confirm the Windows configuration path (basically you just hit the enter key again)

•Next choose to reset password by selecting corresponding number (preselected by default- Illustration 2-4)

•Now at the next screen, choose “Edit user data and passwords” by selection. The default choice is already preselected so just hit the enter key

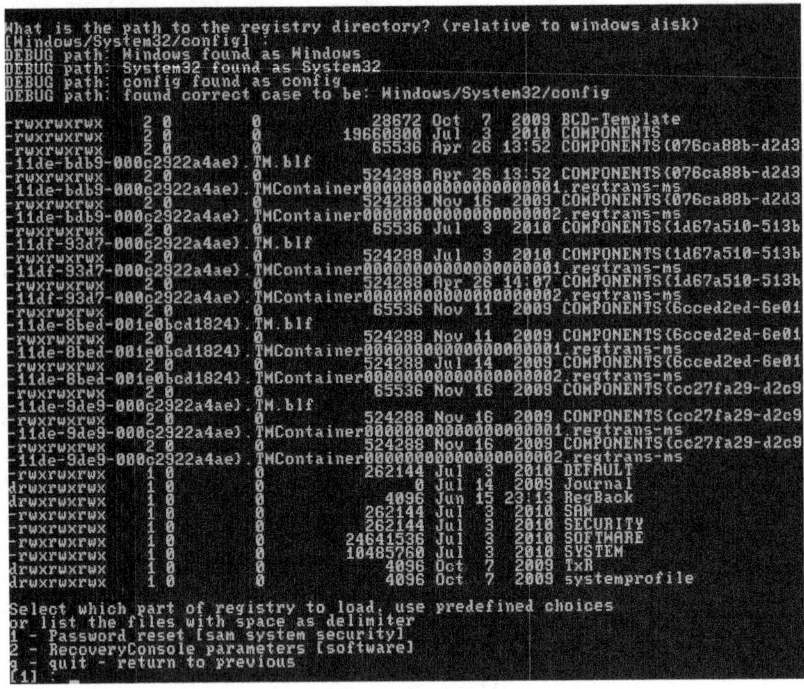

Illustration 2-4

•Next you must type the user name exactly as it appears in the choices and press enter key
•Ensure to use capitalization, hyphens, and underscores if used
•At the next screen choose to "Clear (blank) user password" by selecting the number 1 and hitting the enter key
•If you correctly entered the user name then the next words should read "successfully cleared!"
•Now select "!" on your keyboard (shift key + 1) to begin the process of saving what you have done
•At the next blinking cursor where it reads "What to do?" type the letter "q" to quit
•The computer should read "about to write file(s) back! Do it?" type the letter "y" for yes
•You will see "***Edit Complete*** new run?" select "n" for no.

(Illustration 2-5)

If you have made an error and wish to repeat the process then select “y” for yes to start over. Otherwise, after selecting “no”, remove the CD or USB flash drive and press Ctrl+Alt+Del to reboot your computer. When Windows reboots, log into the original account to create a new password that you'll remember, but is hard for someone else to guess. Illustration 2-5

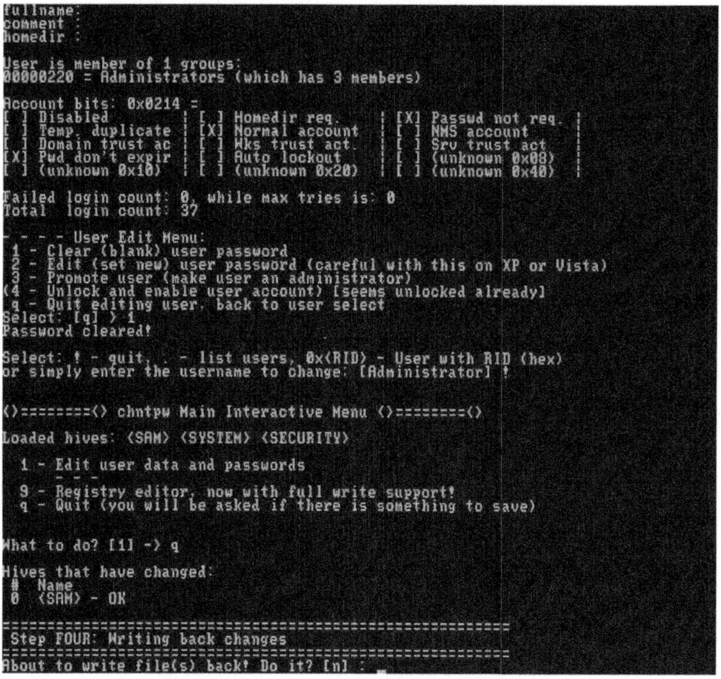

```
Fullname:
comment :
homedir :

User is member of 1 groups:
00000220 = Administrators (which has 3 members)

Account bits: 0x0214 =
[ ] Disabled        | [ ] Homedir req.    | [X] Passwd not req. |
[ ] Temp. duplicate | [X] Normal account  | [ ] NMS account     |
[ ] Domain trust ac | [ ] Wks trust act.  | [ ] Srv trust act   |
[X] Pwd don't expir | [ ] Auto lockout    | [ ] (unknown 0x08)  |
[ ] (unknown 0x10)  | [ ] (unknown 0x20)  | [ ] (unknown 0x40)  |

Failed login count: 0, while max tries is: 0
Total  login count: 37

- - - - User Edit Menu:
 1 - Clear (blank) user password
 2 - Edit (set new) user password (careful with this on XP or Vista)
 3 - Promote user (make user an administrator)
(4 - Unlock and enable user account) [seems unlocked already]
 q - Quit editing user, back to user select
Select: [q] > 1
Password cleared!

Select: ! - quit, . - list users, 0x<RID> - User with RID (hex)
or simply enter the username to change: [Administrator] !

<>========<> chntpw Main Interactive Menu <>========<>

Loaded hives: <SAM> <SYSTEM> <SECURITY>

  1 - Edit user data and passwords
  - - -
  9 - Registry editor, now with full write support!
  q - Quit (you will be asked if there is something to save)

What to do? [1] -> q

Hives that have changed:
 #  Name
 0  <SAM> - OK

=======================================================
 Step FOUR: Writing back changes
=======================================================
About to write file(s) back! Do it? [n] :
```

Chapter Summary

Having strong network security protocols and the safe keeping of important information, should be top priority in today’s world of cyber criminals. Routinely changing your password, updating network access, and ensuring your firewall is up and running are all good practices to start. Losing a password could happen to anyone, but what if we had a backup of all of our passwords? A good way to avoid getting locked out of your computer is to back up your passwords on an external device, such as a USB flash drive or data CD. There are many password retrieval programs on the market that will either break passwords, providing you with the actual password, or simply remove it all together. Most of the current Windows versions have been integrated with security backdoors on hidden partitions to allow for system resets.

The reset sequence completely erases all data and effectively restores your computer back to the factory default condition, which for some, isn't the best solution. Keeping a backup of your operating system is an ideal strategy, but just like the old saying goes….*there are times when the barn door is fixed, only after the horse has run away*. This means that you should put certain safeguards in place to protect the things that are valuable to you to prevent loss. We can take steps to prevent many things from happening to the network systems, but there is no such thing as a computer network ever being 100% secure.

Chapter 3
Effective Methods of Removing Clutter

There are many different methods with which you may remove a malware virus from your computer. Depending on how bad the infection is will determine the probable course of action, but you may also change the order of attack as you see fit. Stopping the virus, or at least slowing it down, is the priority and goal until a suitable antivirus program can be installed. To do this, log into your Windows account as a system administrator and follow these steps:

Windows Versions-All

•Go to your start button

•Type "msconfig" without quotation marks and press your enter key

•Select the tab "services" by clicking on it

•Towards the bottom check the box "Hide all Microsoft services."

•Click on the box that states "Disable all" (afterward there should be no checked boxes)

•Now click on "Apply" at the bottom

•Go to Startup tab and open it

•Click on the button that states "Disable all" and click on "Apply" (boxes should now be empty)

•Now click on "OK"

•When prompted to exit and restart the computer choose "Yes exit and restart"

After completing the above steps and restarting your computer, press the F8 key and choose to boot in "safe mode" to start Windows with just the basic programs and drivers. Safe mode will allow you to make necessary repairs to an operating system while limiting the amount of programs that could possibly

hinder the software or hardware troubleshooting process. In the next steps we will begin to remove temporary, junk, and obsolete registry files that could slow down your antivirus scan. Now that you are signed in safe mode you will need to do the following:
•Click on the Windows Start button and look for "My Computer" (**XP**) or "Computer" (**Vista/ Windows 7**) and open it
•Navigate over to your "C" drive and use your mouse button to **right click** on it once to expose the drop down menu
•Now scroll down and go into "Properties"
•Look for "Disk Cleanup" and open that up
•**Windows 8** and **8.1** users can access "Disk Cleanup" typing into the Search Charm and choose "Free up disk space by deleting unnecessary files"
•Once Disk Cleanup has finished scanning for temporary files, place a check in all of the boxes
•Next click on "Clean up system files" or click "OK" (for later versions)
•A message box will appear asking if you are sure you want to permanently delete these files...click "yes

Once all unnecessary files have been removed, you can close out Disk Cleanup and reboot your computer as you normally would. When you are logged into Windows again you will now begin to take the offensive position to assault the viruses in the most common places of where they hide. Always remember that the best defense is a good offense!

Step by Step Instructions on Virus Removal

You must log into your computer with administrative privileges to make changes to the system's programs and folders. What you will be looking for is a Windows system folder called "Prefetch," which contains small files in this folder about your computer surfing habits as well as programs that you have opened or are currently running in the background. The theory behind Microsoft wanting to store these files is that by doing so it will aid your computer's launching of the programs faster. However, some of these programs running should be deemed malicious and have unfortunately inserted themselves into this very folder for faster loading capabilities. Follow these steps to remove files from the Prefetch folder:

•Go to your Start button and click it

•Scroll over to "My Computer" (for XP users) or "Computer" (for later versions)

•Open up the C: drive

•Scroll down to the "Windows" folder and open

•Navigate down to the "Prefetch" folder and open

•Highlight all files except "ReadyBoot" (Later Versions). Win XP users should highlight all files within the Prefetch folder

•Using the right click option of your Mouse Pad, click once and scroll down the drop down menu to "delete"

•Choose to delete all files, sending them to the Recycle Bin

•Go quickly to the Recycle Bin and right click on the icon (usually located on your desktop).

•Scroll down to "Empty Recycle Bin" and click that option.

•If prompted "Are you sure you want to permanently delete these files?" choose yes.

When repairing computers, I often check in several

locations where I know viruses reside and function as a browser hack. Most viruses that redirect browser change the target box located in the browser's shortcut. To check your browsers target web address destination, go down to Windows Task Bar or wherever you see the internet browser's icon and right click on it. If you can't find your internet browser icon, type the name of your browser into your computer search box, and when your browser is found then right click on it.

How to Configure Computer Security Settings

The most important feature in Windows that you will want to pay close attention too is by far its security settings. All versions of Windows come with built in components that allow you (Administrator) to customize it according to your very own specifications. As a default, and straight out of the box, Windows security features are set at a minimum to provide you with at least some level of protection. To change settings or to ensure that your system is up to speed on all of its protective shielding, you will need to proceed into your control panel (for XP, Windows Vista, 7). For Windows 8 and 8.1, swipe your cursor towards the upper right corner of the desktop screen to expose the Search option then type "Firewall" and open it (then skip down). Once you are in your perspective areas for making the security changes, follow these steps:

Windows XP users

•Once you are in Control Panel, go to "Security Center"

•Ensure that the **Firewall, Automatic Updates**, and **Virus Protection** are all "ON" and green

•To turn any of the three categories listed on or off, click on the drop down arrow. In this case ensure they are set to "ON"

•If your Virus Protection is red because you don't have any protection then we recommend Avast! (Free edition at avast.com)

•If you had to download Avast! , go ahead and finish the install. Once complete, go to your Settings to ensure it's now green

Windows Vista and 7 users

•Once in the Control Panel, go to "System and Security"

•Now click on "Windows Firewall"

•When the page appears, look for "Windows Firewall State" and if it reads "ON" you are good

•If it reads "Off" then navigate over to the left side panel and click "Turn Windows Firewall on or off"
•Under "Home Network" and "Public Network" heading, click on "Turn on Windows Firewall"
•When you have changed the setting or if no changes needed to made, click on "OK" to save
Windows 8 & 8.1 users
•Once you are in "Firewall" setting after following the steps above, ensure that your Firewall is turned "ON"
•If the Firewall is "Off", click on "Turn Windows Firewall on or off"
•When the page appears go under "Home Network" and "Public Network" to change the settings to "On"
Lastly, to save changes, if any, click on "OK" and exit the settings

A Shortcut and a potential automatic fix for any of your Windows computer related problems, is to download the free Microsoft Windows program, "Mr. Fixit." The majority of configuration problems are automatically detected and corrected by using Mr. Fixit. Visit Microsoft support at http://support.microsoft.com/mats/program_install_and_uninstall/en-us knowledgebase webpage to download the program.

Changing Browser Settings

Windows uses Internet Explorer for its web browser by default, and comes preinstalled on all of its operating systems. However, there are many other browsers to choose from that work just as good as or maybe even better than Internet Explorer. For the sake of this topic, and it is assumed that you have current versions of your particular browsers, we will be discussing Internet Explorer and Google Chrome. To optimize protection through your chosen internet browser while offering the best web surfing experience, do the following:

Internet Explorer

Note: There is a shortcut to reset your internet configurations completely back to its original settings by going into the "Advanced" tab and click on "Reset."

•Go to your setting icon located at the top right of your screen
•Next, scroll down to "Internet Options" and click on it
•A box opens displaying the "General" tab
•Now choose to set your web browser's homepage to default setting or whatever homepage you like (ex.www.msn.com)
•Click on the box next to "Delete browsing history on exit"
•Click "Apply" and then "OK"
•Navigate to the top tab in the same window and click on "Connections"
•Scroll down to "LAN settings" and click on it
•Click on the box "Automatically detect settings" or if it is already checked then leave it checked
•Make sure that there are NO other checked boxes in this window then click "OK"
•Take a look at the settings in the "Privacy" tab which is located at the top in the same window
•Check the box "Never allow websites to request your physical

location,"
•Check the box "Turn on **Pop-up blocker**," and "Disable toolbar and extensions when **InPrivate browsing** starts."
•Finally, proceed to the "Security" tab (located at the top) place a checkmark into the box labeled "Enable protected mode."

When you're done making all of the necessary changes to Internet Explorer, click on "Apply" to save all changes made. You should be prompted with the message "You must restart your web browser for changes to take place." Just click on "OK" to restart your browser and verify that all changes have been made and are correct.

Google Chrome, in my opinion, is far superior and feature rich than that of Internet Explorer. Google Chrome has combined the keyword search features of Google into its web browser for superior delivery of websites and search results. Chrome offers faster speeds, easy user interfacing, Apps marketplace (Chrome Web store) better overall security, and Flash Player comes preinstalled on its platform. Oh, did I mention Chrome has faster speeds-I did and speed makes all the difference. Chrome uses a built in prediction search tool to help with your searches, which comes in handy, especially if the wrong spelling to words are being used. As you type into the web search bar, the prediction tool starts to arrange possible websites that you are possibly going to visit. To optimize your internet settings, follow these few steps.

Google Chrome

•Go to the settings icon located at the top corner of your internet page and click on it
•Scroll down to "Settings" and click on it
•Look for the heading "On Startup"
•Scroll down to "Open a specific page or set of pages," click "Set pages"

•In the box that says "Enter URL," type the web address homepage you want to appear on startup (i.e. www.cnn.com)
•If you only want one page to appear, then scroll upward and click on the "X" mark at the end of the grayed box to remove it
•When you have finished adding or removing your web pages, click "OK" to save changes
•Scroll down the page and look for "Search" and choose a search engine that you trust (i.e. Google, Yahoo, Bing, or AOL)

Note: Alternatively, you can choose to reset your browser internet settings to its original condition by scrolling down to "Show Advanced settings" and at the bottom of the page "Reset browser settings" to restore to original condition. If you choose to reset your browser settings, you will lose your preferred homepage and any security changes that you've made. Now close out Google Chrome and reopen it to verify that all of your settings have been applied. If not, repeat the above steps and ensure that you've clicked "Ok" when finished.

Chapter Summary

Malware will thrive in a slow moving computer environment that is full of unnecessary programs and clutter. Taking the time to remove junk files and uninstalling programs that are not needed could significantly increase your computer's response time in warding off cyber attacks. Set Window Updates to automatically download and install at specific times of the day and check browser settings to ensure that your home page is not being redirected. The Control Panel of your operating system plays an integral part in customizing your computer's settings. Other settings regarding internet operations can be changed via settings in whatever web browser you choose. At a minimum, popup blocking should always be enabled and your security protocols should be set to moderate protection. Most antivirus programs offer an internet web security protection feature that scans websites for potential threats before granting access.

Choosing a good web browser could mean the difference of whether or not your computer becomes infected with malware or other types of spyware. Internet Explorer has been plagued with many security problems and deemed by many as the least secure. Google Chrome offers a better level of protection with a more beneficial and user friendly security center that is very easy to understand. Whatever web browser that you choose to use, ensure that you are current with all provided updates and be watchful of messages or Ads that want you to click on them.

Chapter 4:
Master Reset by Model a.k.a Scorched Earth

In this chapter we will discuss methods of restoring your computer to factory default when all else fails, even if you have no Windows Disk. Factory default is basically the condition from which the computer was first purchased and opened for the first time. There are times when there just aren't any other viable options but to start from scratch. This is especially true when data contained on your operating system has been so corrupted, and damage has already been done to a point necessitating a complete reset. Most computers nowadays do not come with restore disks anymore, as the factory image is hidden away in a recovery partition located on the hard drive. I will break down the steps by computer brand name as the model number really will not matter. For example, the steps to reset an HP Laptop will be the same steps taken to reset the HP Desktop - and so on.

The reset procedure includes all models of laptops and desktops under the designated manufacturing company's brand name. The only thing that may change is the order with which to initiate certain commands based on your particular operating system (Vista, Windows 7, 8 and 8.1). The Windows reset option can be used when you want to restore your computer to the original factory image, which is the status as if it were just turned on for the first time, and you don't care about losing your saved data. Remember, most of the time this method is chosen when there are extreme problems with the computer and nothing else seems to work; however, it is always best to back up your computer files regularly.

Also, you will have the option, while doing a master reset, to save or backup your files before proceeding. If you choose to perform this action, follow the steps provided by your computer's built in wizard while resetting to factory default. If you are choosing to completely reset your computer to factory default and save no files, follow the listed directions below by brand name. Make sure you have an ac adapter plugged in (for laptop) during the recovery session. You must press the corresponding keys before your particular computer's logo screen appears. If you miss the allotted time, restart your computer and try again-timing is very important. After powering on your computer, you will need to press specific keys to access the factory default reset mode.

Acer

Windows Vista/Windows 7

•On power up press the "**Alt+F10**" keys simultaneously several times to enter recovery mode

•Next, you should see a long bar that reads "Windows is loading files"

•When the screen is finished loading you will be presented several options. Choose "Restore system to factory default"

•Proceed to next screen that simply states that c: drive will be overwritten, plug in charger, and unplug all else. Click next

•The next screen "Destination Hard Drive Information" confirms where the installation will occur. Click next

•A notice box should appear prompting you that all data will be overwritten. Click OK to proceed

•Be patient. The next screen will show approximate time until completion. The procedure has now begun

•When the system has finished, you can now follow the onscreen prompts to set a new username and password

•You can continue through the customization process to select whatever optional things you like

Acer

Windows 8/8.1

•Power on the computer

•When you get to the login screen look down to the lower right corner and press the start button for options

•Hold down the "**Shift key"** while clicking on **"Restart"** ***and*** keep pressing on the Shift key until it auto restarts

•When the next screen options appear, click on "Troubleshoot"

•Now click on "Reset your PC"

•The next screen will basically state you will lose all data and the computer will be reset to default condition. Click "Next"

•You will now be presented with two options. Choose "Just remove my files" as this is faster

•Next you will be prompted again that your personal files will be removed. Click "Reset"

•Once the computer is fully reset, you will be prompted to set your language, username, and password

Asus

Windows Vista/Windows 7

•Power on your computer and immediately press "F9" and hold down until you see the submenu

•If by pushing "F9" nothing happens, "Boot Booster" maybe enabled and will have to be disabled by pressing "F2" on startup and going into "Boot Options." Next, scroll down to "Boot Booster" and choose disable then press "F10" to save and exit. Once the computer reboots, immediately press and hold"F9" until submenu appears

•Select the operating system (by default just hit enter)

•Starting Windows should be visible while loading
•Next select your language choice. Click "Next"
•Recovery Wizard. Click "Next"
•Went given options of how to install Windows. Choose "Recover Windows to entire HD." Click "Next"
•The Preload Wizard screen should appear. Click "Next"
•On the Preload Wizard screen #2.Click "Finish"
•Windows will begin to reset to factory default status. Be patient. When prompted, enter your new username and password

Asus

Windows 8/8.1

•Power on the computer and immediately press "F9" and hold down for 5-6 seconds or until the submenu appears
•Your PC should now begin to enter recovery option mode
•When the next screen appears, you will have several choices. Choose "Troubleshoot"
•Now when another screen comes up, choose "Reset your PC"
•Next when the new screen appears, choose "Just remove my files"
•You will be presented with a new screen that basically states that you will lose your files. Click "Reset"
• Once the computer is fully reset, you will be prompted to set your language, username, and password

Compaq

Windows Vista/7

•Power on the computer and immediately press "F8" and hold down for 5-6 seconds (some models F10 or F11)
•Setup will begin to load the recovery console (screen should read "Windows is loading files....")
•The next screen that appears will provide you with several

choices to select from, choose "Microsoft System Restore"
•Now choose to "Accept" the option on the next screen (basically everything you have will be overwritten and replaced)
•Continue through the next screen which confirms the last and click "Continue" to begin the process or restoring your PC
•Once restoration has completed, follow the onscreen prompts to re-enter your personal information including new password

Compaq

Windows 8/8.1

•Power on the computer and immediately press the "F11" key once per second until keyboard layout screen appears
•Choose your layout (i.e.; English layout etc…)
•The next screen will be "Choose an option"
•You will choose "Troubleshoot" to rest your PC
•When the next screen appears, choose "Reset your PC"
•Follow the onscreen prompts to revert your computer back to factory default including choosing a name and password

Dell

Windows Vista, Windows 7/8/8.1/

•Power on the computer and immediately press the "F8" key once per second until the "Advanced Boot Menu" appears
•Choose "Repair Your Computer" and click the "Enter" key
•The next screen should load the "Recovery Partition" automatically
•Choose your language and other settings
•Input your Administrative user name and password (or if you have forgotten your password, remove the password with this tool and restart the process. Once password is removed, follow the above instructions again press "OK" to continue through the Administrative password screen

• On the next screen choose "Dell Factory Image Restore" and click "Next"
•Now, choose "Reformat the hard drive and restore system…"click "Yes" and finally click "Next" to reset to factory default
•Follow the onscreen prompts to setup your computer for first use (i.e. username, password, internet, etc...)

EMachines

Windows Vista/Windows 7

•Power on your computer and immediately press "Alt + F10" key simultaneously (some computers you will have to press "F8" to access "Repair Your Computer" option
•Your computer will now boot into the "eRecovery Management" where you will be presented with two options
•Option 1 will be to restore your computer to factory default, whereas option 2 will be to restore and keep all files
•Choose option 1, "Restore Operating System to Factory Default"
•Read the disclaimer that essentially informs you that all stored data will be lost and then click on "Next"
•Accept the default installation directory by clicking "Next" to proceed
•You will be presented with one last warning that all data will be lost and your computer will be restored, click "OK"
•Now your restoration will begin to load, be patient because depending on your hard drive size, this could take awhile
•Follow the onscreen prompts to setup your computer for first time use (i.e. username, password, internet, etc…)

HP

Windows XP

•Power on your computer and immediately press "F10" multiple

times until the Recovery Manager appears
•Choose "Destructive recovery" by clicking "Advanced" and then select "Destructive Recovery", now click "Next"
•Follow the Onscreen prompts to complete the recovery and setup for first time use (i.e. username, password, internet, etc...)

Windows Vista

•Power on your computer and immediately press "F11" multiple times until the Recovery Manager appears
•Recovery Manager will now be visible, click "Next" to continue
•Microsoft Restore screen will open with two options; choose "no, I would like to see other options," now click "Next"
•"System Recovery" will appear with an option if you want to perform a system recovery. Choose "yes" and click "Next"
•The next screen gives another option to backup data, choose "Recover without backing up your files" and select "Next"
•Factory Image Recovery begins.....be patient as this may take awhile
•Once the recovery process has completed, follow the onscreen prompts to setup your computer for first time use (i.e. username, password, internet, etc…)

Windows 7

•Power on your computer and immediately press "F11" multiple times until the Recovery Manager appears
•In the first column, at the bottom of the row, there should be an option "System Recovery," click it
•You will be prompted to back up your files or continue without backing up your files, select "Recover without backing up your files" and click "Next" to continue
•Now you will again be prompted with a warning that all files will be overwritten or deleted….click "OK" to continue
•When the recovery has completed, click "Finish." The computer

will restart and then you can follow the onscreen prompts to setup your computer for first time use (i.e. username, password, internet, etc…)

Windows 8/8.1

•Power on your computer and immediately press "F11" multiple times until "Choose your Keyboard Layout" screen appears
•Choose your keyboard layout
•Now the computer will restart and you should see the "Choose an option" screen
•Select "Troubleshoot" to continue
•Now select "Recovery Manager" to continue
•Once you are at the recovery screen, select the target operating system that you want to restore and click on it
•HP Recovery Wizard appears with three columns, under "I need immediate help" click on "Minimized Image Recovery"
•You will now be prompted to choose a backup option select "Recover without backing up your files" and click "Next"
•The HP Recovery Manager welcome screen will appear, follow the onscreen guide and click "Next" to begin recovery
•Be patient and follow any onscreen prompts….the system will restart several times during this process
•When the recovery is complete, click "Finish" to begin first time setup and registration

Toshiba

Windows Vista/Windows 7

•Power on your computer while holding down the "0" key (Zero) until the computer beeps, then release the key
•Choose yes when prompted to proceed to the system recovery
•Choose to "Recovery of Factory Default Software" and click "Next"

•Choose "Recover to out of box state" and then click "Next"
•Now click "Next" one more time and the recovery process should begin
•Follow the onscreen prompts to complete recovery and first time setup

Windows 8/8.1

•Power on the computer and immediately press the "0" key until keyboard layout screen appears
•Choose your layout (i.e.; English layout etc…)
•The next screen will be "Choose an option"
•You will choose "Troubleshoot" to rest your PC
•When the next screen appears, choose "Reset your PC"
•Follow the onscreen prompts to revert your computer back to factory default including choosing a name and password

Lenovo

Windows 7

•Power on the computer and immediately press the "F11" key until launching the recovery utility screen appears
•The next screen "System Recovery Options" for keyboard select your choice and click "Next"
•Now you will be prompted to enter your username and password, if you have forgotten please see refer back to Chapter 2
•If you don't have a password set, then click "OK" to proceed to the next recovery options screen
•Scroll down to the bottom and select "Lenovo Product Recovery"
•Now you will be prompted by another screen, "Product Recovery," select your preferred language and then click "Next"
•Read and accept the agreement that explains your data will be lost and rest to factory default, then click "Next"
•You will be prompted yet again with a reminder that all data will

be lost and rest, click “Yes” to proceed
•The recovery now begins, be patient as this may take awhile. When recovery is complete click “Finished”
•Finally, follow the onscreen prompts to enter your new user information (i.e. passwords, username, internet, etc…)

Windows 8/8.1
•Power on the computer and press the “F8” (some models “F11”) key until “Advanced boot options” screen appears
•Scroll down to “Repair Your Computer” and press your “Enter” key
•Now choose your default language and click “Next”
•Enter your administrative login credentials and click “OK”
•Now choose the “Lenovo Factory Image Restore,” click “Next”
•Accept the prompt by selecting “Yes” that basically states you want to format the hard drive and restore your computer
•Finally, click “Next” to begin the process of restoring your computer to factory default
•Follow all onscreen prompts for first time use setup and enter your new username, password, and internet connection

Chapter Summary

This chapter dealt with the restoration of Windows operating system and the many different computer manufacturing restore guidelines. Computer manufacturers in the past would provide Windows restore and repair disks, but nowadays the factory restore images are contained within a separate partition. Sometimes it is necessary to completely restore your computer to factory default due to damages caused by malicious programs or simply because of human error. The Scorched Earth method is look upon as the last effort attempted after all else have failed, but there are no real winners in this scenario, especially when entire data systems are lost in the process.

The best solution to minimize the casualties of loss is to have a backup working copy of your hard drive. This can be by using programs like Norton Ghost or by the free method of using a good old fashioned external hard drive. Whichever method you decide works best, your goal should be to establish regular intervals where you create updated images of your working database. In the end, and if you follow these simple rules, the stress of having to have had to format your operating system wouldn't be quite as bad.

Chapter 5

Step by Step Guide to Reinstalling Your Version of Windows

The process for installing Windows is generally the same on every computer, whether it's a laptop or desktop, it maybe that your operating system is so corrupted that a new installation is your only choice. It could also be that a virus has done damage to certain files or programs and has made them all but impossible to repair. There are times where the hidden partition on your hard drive has also become corrupted necessitating the use of a bootable Windows disk or flash drive. For whatever the reasoning, installing a new operating system has now become your only option of getting that computer up and running like new again. I will take you through the procedures of installation and activating your version of Windows, and I have included in this book, all versions of the Windows 7 operating systems for both 32 and 64 bit operating systems.

If you don't know whether or not you have a 32 bit or 64 bit, you can just install the 32 bit (x86) to be on the safe side. The 64 bit operating system is backwards compatible, which means if your system is 64 bit and then you install the 32 bit (x86), it would work just fine. The terms 64 bit and 32 bit are used in reference to the type of processor you have on your motherboard; the difference is speed. A 64 bit computer processor will handle bits of data and tasks more efficiently than that of its counterpart, the 32 bit processor. If you didn't know that you had a 64 bit processor on your computer and you are installing a 32 bit operating system, the 64 bit processor will still work without issue, but not as fast as it intended to.

Ok, so now that we know the basics of the 32 bit vs. 64 bit operating systems, let's jump right in and begin the process of reinstalling your operating system. If you didn't have a working copy of Windows restore disk, but you do have a license key (see License key) for your particular version of Windows, proceed to Chapter 6 to copy the link into your web browser of your specific version that matches your Windows key. The key is located on a sticker on the underside of your laptop or on the rear or your desktop computer. In some instances, the sticker is actually located inside the computer underneath the removable battery.

If your sticker is missing or has become worn to the point that you can't read it anymore and Windows still can boot up, you can download the free program, Magic Jelly Bean (Product Key Finder), which can find and display your Windows product key. Once you have located your Windows product key, write it down and put it aside for when it's needed. Follow the instructions below after you have created a boot disk that matches your product key. For example, if you have a Windows 7 Home Premium, it doesn't matter if processor is x86 or x64 (Product key is neutral); you have to download the operating system Windows 7 Home Premium.

Similarly, if it's Professional, Starter, Enterprise, or Ultimate, versions of Windows the installation process is the same. However, Windows 7 Enterprise will have to be installed by requesting the 90 day free trial file directly from Microsoft by logging in and requesting the link for download. Once you have the downloaded file, you can burn the file image to a DVDR or bootable USB drive, and insert your particular product key into the boxes when prompted during the installation process. To begin, and it is assuming that you have already followed the instruction on creating a boot disk, insert your disk into the DVD drive (or USB if flash drive) of your computer or laptop. Next,

press the key that works with your computer for changing the boot order. For most computers it's "F12" for boot options, or "F2" to go into the bios and change from there.
•You should be prompted with an onscreen message "Press any key to boot from CD or DVD" which also includes USB
•Now, press any key located on your keyboard to start the installation process
•Once the computer boots from the selected drive, the installation will begin by loading windows installation files
•The next screen you see will show the Windows Logo and a message will appear "Starting Window"
•You will now be prompted with a menu that essential tells you to select your language and time zone etc.., click "Next"
•Next, a new "Install Windows" screen appears, click "Install now" to proceed
•Setup is starting…screen will be visible by this point
•Select the Windows operating system that you have the product key for (Home Premium, Professional, Ultimate, etc...) **Also remember that if you don't know if your computer is x64 or x86, choose "x86"**
•Read the terms and check the box to "I accept the license terms" (for your version of Windows) and click "Next"
•You will now see a window with the question of "Which type of installation do you want?" click "Custom"
•On the next screen "Where do you want to install Windows?" choose the largest partition and click "Next"
•Windows will now begin to install, which could take up to an hour depending on the speed of your computer. Be patient...
•Wait for it……..
•Wait for it……..
•Wait for it……..

•Now, Windows may restart several times during the installation phase, but it won't require you to do anything yet
•Once the installation is almost complete, you should see a screen, "Setup is updating registry settings"
• The screen, "Setup is starting services" will appear……and next your computer will be configured for first use

By the time the entire process is completed, Windows would have checked and configured most of your hardware devices and updated many of the programs that came with your version of Windows. When the installation is fully completed, you will be asked to provide a username and password. Follow the onscreen prompts to enter all relevant information including internet connections. There may be times when you have to go to your computer's manufacturer website to get the latest drivers and updates. To ensure that you have the latest device drivers needed for your computer, follow these steps to check "Device Manager" to verify that all drivers are present:

•Click the start menu icon located in the lower left side of your screen, in the "Search programs and files" box, type "Device Manager"
•When the search has completed, scroll up and click on, "Device Manager"
•If there are question marks (?) next to a driver, you must go to your computer's manufacturer website to update drivers
•Alternatively, you can search your "Windows.old" folder for missing drivers too
• (You can also use another computer to download all drivers to a USB flash drive to install on the destination PC)
•From the manufacturer's website, download the correct drivers by first entering your computer's model number
•Now choose your installed operating system and bit (32bit/x86

or 64bit)

•Scroll down to “Network” or any other category to download and install any missing drivers

•Follow the onscreen prompts provided by the hardware driver manufacturer

Be patient while searching for drivers for your operating system, most drivers can be obtained by allowing Windows to search its vast database automatically for missing driver files. If you don’t feel comfortable downloading drivers from the manufacturer’s website, there are programs out there such as Driver Detective or Driver Easy that will search and obtain your drivers for you.

Downloading and Installing optional programs

When repairing a computer after a fresh install of Windows, whether by way of resetting the pc to factory default or through a clean install, I go to Filehippo.com which is considered by many, a one stop website for all software. Filehippo contains all free programs which are used by the professionals to protect, optimize, and clean your computer — for a fee. I mean most people will attempt to sell ice to Eskimos if they could; most of them often succeed too. The first line of defense for your new operating system, besides the Windows Firewall, is a good antivirus program. There are many antivirus programs out there, but as stated earlier, some are better than others. I personally recommend Avast! for the simple at home user as well as for light business use. There are, however, two editions one being free and the other, paid. It's your choice as to whether you want to pay for something that is just as good as the free version and works in conjunction with your Windows built in safeguards. Once you install Avast! (Free edition or paid), the program automatically searches for new virus definitions and begins a scan as soon as the program opens. The wonderful thing about Avast! is that it updates several times a day without you having to do anything, as well as quietly running in the background and audibly informing the user that it has been updated. After you have decided which version of the antivirus you're going with, download the next program that will aid you in optimizing your computer's performance; the program is called CCleaner.

CCleaner is a really nice piece of software that cleans registry, removes unwanted programs, can remove (bloatware) unnecessary startup programs from running, and removes system clutter. CCleaner can scan for traces of programs that were once used on your computer and delete those unused files that were left behind. Having a computer full of obsolete program fragments will ultimately slow your overall PC's performance. You can even set CCleaner to run at startup to clean preselected areas of your hard drive, removing old browsing history data from the internet as well as old temporary files and cookies. There are several other handy features of CCleaner as well; for example, you can set CCleaner to uninstall a program and securely wipe all passwords and digital footprints ever made on a computer. This is a powerful tool and should be used with caution, and the best part of it all is that it's *free.* The list of great programs that Filehippo has to offer is endless, especially if you're ever in need of a remote repair. There's a program, also free, that allows you to connect or be connected to someone else's computer for PC repair. The benefits of remote access are limitless and great for cost saving and other added conveniences; the program is called TeamViewer.

TeamViewer has saved me tons of cash in gas alone. Not having to go out in the middle of the night to perform a software related repair onsite as opposed to over the internet is the top reason why I choose this program. I believe that every computer should have a quick access remote program for just this type of reason. What happens if your Microsoft Office program won't open in the middle of the evening, just when you've got to get that last PowerPoint presentation completed? These types of problems are most often due to registry errors or corrupted data files, but with TeamViewer, someone who's computer literate could remote in to repair it. I have also compiled a list of programs that you'll need upon reinstalling your operating system, of which I have only named a few. There won't be any Adobe Reader or Flash Player installed, you will have to go to each of the vendor's website to manually ask for them. Earlier in the book I gave a brief overview of the best updates you can install, Windows Updates. Make sure your computer is configured to download these crucial security fixes and patches to avoid system hang-ups and blue screening.

A good practice is to keep all of your product keys in two places, both inside and outside, but together for easy access and safe storage. If you haven't already downloaded the free Magic Jelly Bean (Product Key Finder), now is a good time. When you download the key finder program, open Notepad, which is located in your "Accessories" folder, and record each key found, but save the document to a flash drive as well as in My Documents folder of your computer. This way, if you ever need to reinstall your operating system again, you can just print out all of your program products codes from one place. Cloning your own hard drive or creating an image of your hard drive is also a must, especially with the understanding that all things will eventually come to an end. There are several free programs out there that are quite good at making both images and clones of your hard drive, which also replicates existing programs already installed. Some of us buy used computers because they may come with software programs already installed, but what happens if your hard drive began to fail? This is where a cloned hard drive would come into play, offering you an exact copy from the point that you cloned the drive. We are recommending the free program, Clonezilla, which can make a clone of hard drives with ease. If you are new to cloning, then follow the guidelines outlined at Clonezilla.org. At the very least, you should always backup your data regularly either online using programs such as the paid Norton Online Backup or other programs for free listed in the next section.

Tweaking Your Computer

To "Tweak" or not to "Tweak" is the million dollar question. First off, what is tweaking? Well, it's a cool way of saying speeding up your computer or optimizing your computer's performance. All computers, both new and old, have excessive amounts of bloatware that will essentially rob your computer of its full capabilities. Most often times than not, a computer is shipped with programs from third party vendors that would love for you to give them a try. When we install these programs, even if we never use them, they take up unnecessary space and waste your CPU processing power. The first step in speeding up your PC is to uninstall all programs that you don't use and don't even know how they got there. However, in doing so you must be very careful as to not uninstall important programs that Windows need to operate correctly. Once you have determined which programs, if any, are candidates for removal, proceed to uninstall them using CCleaner. When all unnecessary programs have been uninstalled, run registry cleaner, to remove all traces of the program files that were most likely left behind. Follow these steps to perform a computer optimization:

Uninstalling Programs

•In CCleaner on the left side tab selection, click "Tools"
•The "Uninstall" box opens up
•Click one time to highlight the program that you wish to remove
•On the right side, click "Run Uninstaller"
•Another box appears with the uninstaller wizard; follow the onscreen prompts to uninstall the program…

Junk Removal

•Download CCleaner and open it when it's done downloading

•Close all internet browsers

•On the left side tabs, click "cleaner," and put a check mark in the following boxes: Temporary Internet Files, History, Cookies, Recently Typed URLs, Index.dat files, Autocomplete Form History, Recent Documents, Run (in Start Menu), Other Explorer MRUs, Thumbnail Cache, Taskbar Jump Lists, Empty Recycle Bin, Temporary Files, Clipboard, Memory Dumps, Chkdsk File Fragments, Windows Log Files, DNS Cache, Font Cache, and Old Prefetch data

•Now, click "Run Cleaner, "

•A box will warn you that "This process will permanently delete files from your system. Are you sure you wish to proceed?" check the box "Do not show me this message again," and click "OK" to continue

•CCleaner now begins to clean all areas that you have checked; be patient as this may take awhile

•When CCleaner completes the process, click "Run Cleaner" again"

• Once that cycle of cleaning is complete, click "Run Cleaner" again. Repeat until you see a message "0 bytes removed

Registry Cleaning

•While still in CCleaner, click on the "Registry" tab located on the left side

•Next, click on "Scan for Issues"

•Once the scan has completed, click on "Fix selected issues…"

•A new box with appear asking "Do you want to backup changes to the registry?" click "No"

•When the next message box appears, choose "Fix All Selected Issues" and when complete click "Close"

•Repeat this process until the message "No issue were found" is displayed

Startup Programs

•To remove unnecessary startup programs from CCleaner, click "Tools" in the left side tab and scroll down to "Startup"
•Right click on all programs except your antivirus and wireless connection, then click "Disable"
•Once you're done, exit the program and restart your computer
Note: Disabling the programs from starting does NOT uninstall them. Once you open a disabled program, it can reinsert itself as startup program and the process of disabling will have to be repeated

---

Free Product Key Finders

I have compiled a list of 10 product key finders that will work for all versions of Windows. All of the programs are very good at finding your activation key numbers in the event that yours are either unreadable or are lost. Just click on any link below to download and install; all programs are free.

- Magic Jelly Bean
- Belarc Advisor
- Winkeyfinder
- LicenseCrawler
- ProduKey
- WinGuggle
- MSKeyViewer Plus
- Product Key Finder
- SIW Home
- Windows Product Key Finder Professional

Belarc Advisor is our top choice due to its ease of use along with the powerful ability to sniff out a multitude of program keys. However, they all do well at finding Windows XP through Windows 8.1 serial product keys at the very least.

Chapter Summary

In this chapter, we addressed the various methods of reinstalling your version of Windows all the way through downloading programs and finding your licensed product keys. It is very important to routinely clean your Windows registry as well to greatly increase your PC's Performance. Removing junk files can increase your computer's processing power, thus efficiently dedicating the needed CPU memory towards running your antivirus program. You should always backup your hard drive using known and safe programs such as Clonezilla, which is free, or a paid alternative like Norton Ghost. Backing up your data to an external source is highly advisable; options include: external hard drive, USB flash drive, or Cloud-based systems (Norton Ghost). Once you backup your files, routinely update your backup data to keep a current up to date image of your operating system. Storing your passwords in safe location, such as on a USB flash drive, will prevent the need of having to pay for costly password retrieval services.

Chapter 6

Windows Repair Files (All Languages)

Choose the appropriate Windows installation and repair file for which you have a valid product key. Microsoft has partnered with Digital River hosting provider to offer these free and legal OEM installation programs. They are only for individuals that have already purchased a computer, but came with no restore disk. Also, downloads are for those individuals that have purchased a computer that came with Windows installed, but the hidden partition has become damaged or corrupted. To begin, you will need a blank DVDR (not DVDRW), as well as a CD/DVD burning program such as "Imgburn."

Windows 7 SP1 ISO Download Links including English and Foreign Language Versions

•http://msft.digitalrivercontent.net/win/X17-58996.iso Windows 7 Home Premium 32Bit
•http://msft.digitalrivercontent.net/win/X17-58997.iso Windows 7 Home Premium 64Bit
•http://msft.digitalrivercontent.net/win/X17-59183.iso Windows 7 Professional 32Bit
•http://msft.digitalrivercontent.net/win/X17-59186.iso Windows 7 Professional 64Bit
•http://msft.digitalrivercontent.net/win/X17-24394.iso Windows 7 Ultimate x86 English
•http://msft.digitalrivercontent.net/win/X17-24395.iso Windows 7 Ultimate x64 English
•http://msft.digitalrivercontent.net/win/X17-24284.iso Windows 7 Professional x86 Finnish
•http://msft.digitalrivercontent.net/win/X17-24285.iso Windows 7 Professional x64 Finnish

•http://msft.digitalrivercontent.net/win/X17-24286.iso Windows 7 Professional x86 French
•http://msft.digitalrivercontent.net/win/X17-24287.iso Windows 7 Professional x64 French
•http://msft.digitalrivercontent.net/win/X17-24288.iso Windows 7 Professional x86 German
•http://msft.digitalrivercontent.net/win/X17-24289.iso Windows 7 Professional x64 German
•http://msft.digitalrivercontent.net/win/X17-24296.iso Windows 7 Professional x86 Italian
•http://msft.digitalrivercontent.net/win/X17-24297.iso Windows 7 Professional x64 Italian
•http://msft.digitalrivercontent.net/win/X17-24302.iso Windows 7 Professional x86 Norwegian
•http://msft.digitalrivercontent.net/win/X17-24303.iso Windows 7 Professional x64 Norwegian
•http://msft.digitalrivercontent.net/win/X17-24306.iso Windows 7 Professional x86 Portuguese
•http://msft.digitalrivercontent.net/win/X17-24307.iso Windows 7 Professional x64 Portuguese
•http://msft.digitalrivercontent.net/win/X17-24318.iso Windows 7 Professional x86 Spanish
•http://msft.digitalrivercontent.net/win/X17-24319.iso Windows 7 Professional x64 Spanish
•http://msft.digitalrivercontent.net/win/X17-24320.iso Windows 7 Professional x86 Swedish
•http://msft.digitalrivercontent.net/win/X17-24321.iso Windows 7 Professional x64 Swedish
•http://msft.digitalrivercontent.net/win/X17-24328.iso Windows 7 Professional K x86 Korean
•http://msft.digitalrivercontent.net/win/X17-24329.iso Windows 7 Professional K x64 Korean

After downloading the correct .ISO file, use Imgburn or CD BurnerXP to create a bootable DVD. Always use high quality DVD+R media and the slowest burn speed (4x or 6x) for best results. There are screen shots for reference on how to burn a CD or DVD at http://www.imgburn.com/index.php?act=screenshots. Once you have downloaded, burned, and installed your version of Windows, you must go to "Device Manger" to verify all drivers are present. If not, go to your computer manufacture's support web site and check for Windows 7 drivers for your specific model number. If there are Windows 7 drivers, then download to a folder on your hard drive and install all of them, starting with the Motherboard/Chipset drivers, SATA, LAN, Audio, USB, Graphics, Webcam, Etc., and so on.

See: list of Computer Manufacturer's support sites: http://windows.microsoft.com/en-US/windows/help/contact-support/computer-manufacturers

---

Optional Program Files and Websites

Cloud-Based Hard drive Space

•Google Drive

Password Breaking

•Ophcrack Live CD

Virus Protection

•Avast! Free Antivirus

•Malwarebytes

Product Key Locator

•Magic Jelly Bean (Product Key Finder)

•Belarc Advisor

•Winkeyfinder

•LicenseCrawler

•ProduKey

•WinGuggle

•MSKeyViewer Plus

•Product Key Finder

•SIW Home

•Windows Product Key Finder Professional

Websites

•Avast.com

•Filehippo.com

•Teamviewer.com

•Malwarebytes.com

•Magicjellybean.com

•Belarc.com

•Winkeyfinder.com

•Siw-home-edition.software.informer.com

Glossary of Computer Terms

A

Access Point- is a device, such as a wireless router, that allows wireless devices to connect to a network.

Antivirus- Is a software program capable of defending a computer system from malicious code.

B

Backdoor- is a hidden way of gaining access to a computer or network system.

Backup- is a copy of an original file or program.

Bloatware- Bloatware is a program that utilizes large amounts of computer resources unnecessarily.

Botnets-Is a group of computers that are slaves, or have become compromised and are controlled by a hacker to infect other systems.

C

Computer hackers- Someone that looks for security breaches to exploit in a computer system or network.

Computer Virus- A software program, like a human virus, that is capable of reproducing itself, and capable of causing damage to network systems.

D

Database- Is a file system that stores information.

Device Driver- A program written that allows software and installed hardware to communicate.

Device Manager- A program that categorizes all installed hardware on the operating system

E

End User-An end user is the person that a software program or hardware device is designed for.

F

Firewall- A computer firewall regulates the type of data that can pass through it and provides a safety barrier between computer user and unauthorized user

G

Gigabit- (bit) is most often used to measure data transfer rates of local networks and input/output connections.

H

Hard disk- A computer storage unit that contains all information relevant to an operating system and its user profiles.

I

InPrivate Browsing- A browsing filter that blocks the computer user's digital footprint; thus, allowing for a more private internet surfing experience.

ISO Image- A virtual CD or DVD image file encoded to emulate an actual disk drive

J

K

Keylogger- Is a program that captures keystrokes on a computer.

L

M

Malware, derived from the word **malicious software**, is software created to steal information and disrupt computer systems.

N

Network- When you have two or more computers connected to each other, you have a network.

O

Operating System- Is a software platform that communicates with the hardware and allows other programs to run.

P

Pop-up Blocker- A browser setting that prohibits new windows, primarily advertising, from appearing

Program-A program is executable software that runs on a computer.

Q

R

Router- This is a hardware device that routes data (hence the name) from a local area network (LAN) to another network connection.

S

Safe Mode- Safe Mode is a way for the Windows operating system to run with the minimum system files necessary.

T

Trojans- (Also a Trojan horse) is a software program that masquerades as regular programs, such as games, disk utilities, and even antivirus programs.

U

Username- is a name that uniquely identifies someone on a computer system.

V

Virus Definition- Is a binary pattern (a string of ones and zeros) that identifies a specific virus. By checking a program or file against a list of virus definitions, antivirus software can determine if the program or file contains a virus.

W

Windows Updates- A distribution method by which the latest security patches from Microsoft can be delivered to a computer or networking system.

X

X86- x86 is the generic name for Intel processors released after the original 8086 processor.

Y

Z

Zip File- A compressed file.

Bibliography

Avast! (n.d.) Retrieved June 10, 2014, from http://download.cnet.com/Avast-Free-Antivirus-2014/3000-2239_4-10019223.html?part=dl-85737&subj=dl&tag=button

Change how Windows installs or notifies you about updates. (2014). Retrieved June 1, 2014, from http://windows.microsoft.com/en-us/windows/change-windows-update-installation-notification#1TC=windows-7

Christensson, P. (2014, June 1) The Tech Terms Computer Dictionary (Glossary of Terms) Retrieved from: http://www.techterms.com

Configure WPA wireless security for home networks. (2014). Retrieved June 9, 2014, from http://windows.microsoft.com/en-us/windows-xp/help/networking/configure-wpa-wireless-security

Is my pc running the 32 bit or 64 bit version of Windows? (n.d.) Retrieved June 11, 2014, from http://windows.microsoft.com/en-us/windows7/find-out-32-or-64-bit

Filehippo. (2004) Retrieved June 01, 2014, from http://www.filehippo.com/download_ccleaner

Microsoft Digital River Downloads (n.d.) Retrieved June 11, 2014, from https://www2.downloadoffice2010.microsoft.com/usa/registerkey.aspx?culture=en-US&ref=backup

Mr. Fix It (n.d.) Retrieved June 10, 2014, from http://support.microsoft.com/kb/283673

Nordahl-Hagen, Petter (n.d.). Chntpw Remove, bypass, unlock and reset forgotten Windows password. Retrieve from http://www.chntpw.com/download/

Piriform CCleaner (n.d.) Retrieved June 11, 2014, from http://www.piriform.com/ccleaner/download

RedOne, Mimiguy2018, Maniac, Colecrane (n.d). Retrieved June 1, 2014 from Wiki how: http://www.wikihow.com/Disable-Popup-Blockers

S., Leah (2012). Windows 8 Changing a Microsoft Windows Account Password. Retrieved from https://kb.wisc.edu/helpdesk/page.php?id=27374

Kamluk, Vitaly (2013). Kaspersky Security Bulletin 2013. Corporate Threats. Retrieve from http://www.securelist.com/en/analysis/204792317/Kaspersky_Security_Bulletin_2013_Corporate_threats

TeamViewer (n.d.) Retrieved June 09, 2014, from http://www.teamviewer.com/en/index.aspx

The Magic Jelly Bean (n.d.) Retrieved June 11, 2014, from http://www.magicaljellybean.com/keyfinder/

Turn Windows Firewall on or off. (2014). Retrieved June 9, 2014, from http://windows.microsoft.com/en-us/windows/turn-windows-firewall-on-off#turn-windows-firewall-on-off=windows-7

Turn User Account Control on or off. (2014). Retrieved June 9, 2014, from http://windows.microsoft.com/en-us/windows/turn-user-account-control-on-off#1TC=windows-7

Windows Firewall from Start to finish (n.d.) Retrieved from http://windows.microsoft.com/en-us/windows-8/windows-firewall-from-start-to-finish

Windows 7 USB/DVD download tool (2014). Retrieved June 10, 2014, from http://www.microsoftstore.com/store/msusa/html/pbPage.Help_Win7_usbdvd_dwnTool

Understanding Windows Firewall Settings (n.d.) Retrieved June 10, 2014 from http://windows.microsoft.com/en-us/windows/understanding-firewall-settings#1TC=windows-7

32 bit and 64 bit Windows: Frequently asked questions (n.d.) Retrieved June 11, 2014, from http://windows.microsoft.com/en-us/windows/32-bit-and-64-bit-windows#1TC=windows-7

About the Author

Beanie L. Yvonne is a degreed and long time computer repair tech, specializing in Information Technology (I.T.) Networking as well as software engineering. Being a trusted source for Windows repair issues, Beanie has often consulted large and small businesses in networking and computer related needs. Being motivated to help the "little guy", she has been known in the community to offer free computer repair services for the aged and disabled. Currently, Beanie lives in south suburban Homewood, Illinois. Bike riding, horseback riding, archery, and walking are some of her passions.

If you would like more information, please email beanieyvonne@hotmail.com. I am very grateful for your decision to purchase my book, and I would be equally appreciative for your review for me as well. Thank you once again!

Printed in Great Britain
by Amazon